DEFEATING DEPRESSION

You Can Be a VICTOR, Not a Victim!

by
BEN FERRELL

Defeating Depression: You Can Be a Victor, Not a Victim!
ISBN: 978-1-685730-15-4

Published by Word & Spirit Publishing
P.O. Box 701403
Tulsa, OK 74170

Unless otherwise indicated, all Scripture quotations are taken from the *New King James Version* of the Bible. Copyright © 1982 by Thomas Nelson, Inc. Used by permission. All rights reserved.

Scripture quotations marked AMP are taken from the *Amplified Bible*. Copyright © 1954, 1958, 1962, 1964, 1965, 1987 by The Lockman Foundation. Used by permission. All rights reserved.

Cover and Text Design: Lisa Simpson
SimpsonProductions.net

DEDICATION

To Kelly—my wife, soul mate, and the love of my life, who has been my "rock" of support over the years. I am so grateful for you being such a stabilizing factor for me and our children through the ups and downs of life. "Kelly's in My Heart."

To my awesome adult children—Parker, Emily, Eli, and John—who have brought me so much joy and have suffered with me through troubled times. I am forever grateful for you.

To Noah, around whom I can never be depressed, and to all my other precious grandchildren: Samuel, Ayla, Elizabeth, and more to come.

ACKNOWLEDGEMENTS

Our heavenly Father, the Lord Jesus, the Holy Spirit—the Almighty Trinity. Your mercies are new every morning. Without Your goodness and mercy following me all the days of my life, I would be nothing.

To the wonderful friends who have been there and prayed for me: Tim Cameron, Hans Helmerich, Paul Brothers, and our "Band of Brothers." What a difference you've made in my life.

To Keith Wheeler: thanks for being my friend and letting me "walk" with you and the cross around the world.

To Jim and Betsy Williams: thanks for your friendship and support.

To Allen and Ruth Mather, for keeping me close to my first love—Jesus.

To the amazing clients, teammates, and associates of BMCFerrell: You have given me the greatest job in the world. Thank you, Ken and Lynette Hagin, Bayless and Janet Conley, Rick and Denise Renner, Dave and Joyce Meyer—the list goes on.

To Clift and Kathleen Richards—pastors, prayer warriors, and friends through thick and thin.

To Keith Provance, an inspiration to me for many years and who has been responsible for bringing so many writers' messages to the world through book publishing. Truly an unsung hero of the faith.

Special thanks to the Ray and Kathy Pinson Family Foundation for their dear friendship and support.

To each and every reader: I feel your pain, have prayed for you many times, and will continue to pray for you to be a victor!

TABLE OF CONTENTS

Chapter 1

~

WHAT'S THIS ALL ABOUT?

I GET IT. YEP. I REALLY DO. If you or someone you love is dealing with depression, I understand. Depression is a *beast*. It has recently surpassed cancer, heart disease, COVID, and other deadly diseases as the number-one cause of disability in the world.[1]

Depression—or any mental-health challenge—can be very isolating, but I want you to know, you are not alone. Many well-known, successful people and countless others have suffered with this malady. Winston Churchill, former prime minister of the United Kingdom, struggled with it. He called it, "the black dog."

Depression is much more than simply the blues or a feeling of sadness. It is an overwhelming sense of hopelessness, a profound insecurity, and a darkness that can consume your thoughts, feelings, and entire outlook on life. Its cousins—anxiety and panic—can gang up on you and make you feel like your whole world is falling apart, that nothing will end well, including your own life. You wonder, "*OMG! What's going to happen to me?*"

The reason I understand is that I, too, have dealt with depression all my life. Thankfully, I have overcome many episodes. I truly understand if this is what you are going through. I am not a mental-health professional or a physician; I am simply someone on a mission to help people who have these challenges to realize that they, too, can overcome. In the midst of your battle, I want to be your friend. I will share my story and some of the things I have learned that have helped me tame the black dog.

In my journey, I have realized that most people don't understand. When trying to explain it to someone who has not experienced it, I have found that it is nearly impossible to describe, especially when I am in the midst of an episode. I thank God for every mental-health professional who has dedicated his or her life to helping people deal with mental-health issues. However, if the professional hasn't experienced it personally, he or she doesn't really "get it" on an emotional or heart basis. The professional can match symptoms "by the book" and diagnose via the facts, statistics, and research. He or she can prescribe medications on a hit-and-miss basis, but if the person has never been swallowed up in the black hole, it's impossible for him or her to truly understand.

I have gone to a few mental-health counselors over the decades and read much from their books and publications. The only one that I felt really understood was a doctor I went to in Santa Fe, New Mexico. This doctor was an MD, a Doctor of Chinese Medicine, and a Doctor of Naturopathic Medicine. He is the most educated physician I have ever met.

He told me, "Ben, there is no pain like the pain your brain can cause in an episode of depression, anxiety, or panic." Bingo! I had finally found someone who got it! What a relief it was just finding someone who understood.

This excruciating pain is why so many precious people commit suicide as a result of depression. They think that they simply can't take the pain any longer and choose a permanent solution to a temporary problem. My heart breaks for them and anyone who is going through this experience. Not only does my heart break for them, I absolutely *hate* this disease—so much so that I have dedicated my life, my music, my time, and my energy to help those who suffer.

Friend, I am passionate about easing your pain and helping you experience peace. Yes, it is possible to overcome depression, and I pray this book will be a blessing to you or someone you love. Come walk with me through these pages. If nothing else, you will find someone who does understand what you are going through, and I will tell you from experience, *everything is going to be OK.*

Chapter 2

~

MY STORY

THE GREATEST LESSON I HAVE LEARNED through a life-time of dealing with depression is that no matter how terrible it might feel or how hopeless it seems, you can get through it. As my precious mom would tell me, "This, too, shall pass." I have found that to be true.

Through even the worst episodes, God's amazing grace has carried me. Even when I didn't have the strength to get out of bed or I felt like finding a hole and crawling into it, God's grace has seen me through, every single time. Despite all of the episodes, He has given me a productive life and much happiness. I want you to know that He is carrying you now, even as you read these words. Yes, your heavenly Father understands. Know this: if you are suffering now, the good grace of Jesus is undergirding you and carrying you through. You may not feel it or "hear Him" during this time, but *He is there with you!* And yes, this, too, *shall* pass.

I was born into a good family in the mountains of eastern Kentucky, where my dad coached high-school football. We moved to Lexington when I was about five years old. My mom and dad were solid people, and I was the middle son of three boys. My mom told me I was the happiest baby—always smiling and engaging—and people were attracted to me because I was naturally happy and enthusiastic. A natural athlete, I liked playing all sports and participating in many outdoor activities.

As I look back, however, I can see where the early signs of depression began. *I had no confidence.* Although I was not bad looking as a teenager, I never thought any girl would be interested in me. Although I was a good athlete and did well in pick-up games or casual competition with my friends, when it came to organized sports, I had no confidence. I was down on myself and only barely made the football, baseball, and basketball teams.

For some reason, I also was prone to accidents and sickness. Through my kindergarten years as a toddler, I suffered from asthma. I remember not being able to breathe and the panic it brought on as I would be rushed to the hospital in the middle of an attack. Then, between the ages of eight and eighteen, I had a major surgery every year.

When I was eight, I had appendicitis and my appendix ruptured. At that time, we didn't have the antibiotics we do today, so it was life threatening. I had an appendectomy. Then, ten days later, while in critical condition, I had another surgery to remove the poison that had been released into my system. Miraculously, the poison had collected right where my original incision was, and it was easy for the doctor to remove it. I say it was miraculous, because the poison could have collected in my brain, lungs, or heart, any of which would have been fatal.

Then the surgeries continued—a tonsillectomy, three surgeries on an ear from chronic infections, repairs from sports injuries, etc. Despite these challenges, I was president of my junior-high-school class, was a leader in my youth group, and had a rock-and-roll band that played music by the Beatles, Beach Boys, James Taylor, and others. Then, at age sixteen, during the Jesus Movement of the 1970s, I had a dramatic encounter with the Holy Spirit and became a leader in a group that led many young people to Christ. (See, I told you, the grace of God can carry you through!)

Because I was a new Christian who had radically experienced the presence of God, I moved to Tulsa, Oklahoma, to attend Oral Roberts University, a leading Christian university. At that time, Oral Roberts was still alive and was president of the school. He taught a course every Thursday night called, *The Holy Spirit and You*. It was my favorite class, and Oral became my spiritual father. I loved going to chapel, attending classes, playing intermural sports, among other things. I eventually became a regular chapel singer and was a favorite of President Roberts's, because I was unique in that I played both the guitar and the harmonica and sang "Jesus music."

So, life should have been great! However, many nights I found myself in my dorm room with what I now know were episodes of depression. It was horrible, but no one talked about depression back then. I figured it was homesickness. I did find that one thing that brought relief was when I expressed my feelings by playing my guitar and singing in my dorm room. I also had a wonderful roommate, David Stearman, who taught me much about life, music, and songwriting.

One night, while suffering in despair, I wrote the song, "Lifeline," which ended up being recorded in Nashville on my first album. The lyrics reveal how desperate I was during those depressive episodes:

Throw me the Lifeline Brother,
Feels like I'm going under.
Help me see just where I'm going.
Tell me the sun is shinin',
Tell me no dark clouds are linin' the sky,
Help me feel the gentle breeze a blowin'.

For I have lost the vision deep within my soul
And I need You just to help me make it.
I am sick at heart and You can make me whole
And with Your strength my Friend,
I know that I can make it.

bencares.com

Over these many years since college, I have experienced many episodes of depression. Unlike asthma, it was not something I "grew out of," neither have I experienced a miraculous healing or "deliverance" that cured me once and for all. I have, however, learned how to overcome and sometimes, by sheer grit and determination, I have not let depression dominate or destroy my life. On the contrary, as I have said, it has been God's grace that has helped me defeat it so that I have lived a fulfilling and productive life. With this book, I want to share with you the ways in which I have dealt with depression and how I have learned to "bark back" at the ole black dog when he shows up growling.

Chapter 3

WHAT IS THE CAUSE?

DEPRESSION IS COMPLICATED AND CAN BE multifaceted. It can be spiritual. It can be a result of childhood or combat trauma, resulting in Post-Traumatic Stress Disorder (PTSD). It can be biological (chemical). It can be a result of an undisciplined thought life. Regardless, it is a disease. It is vital to understand that depression is not who you *are*. It doesn't define you. You are not a victim. It shouldn't be your identity. Most importantly, please know that *it is not your fault.* Even in the case of an undisciplined thought life, you may need help recognizing a faulty mindset and replacing it with true, positive thoughts.

Earlier in my adult life, it was difficult for me because I was and still am a part of a faith community that, until recent years, hasn't understood or even acknowledged depression as a disease. Some of the ministers I listened to would make statements like, "I've never been depressed a day in my life," or "I refuse to be down even one day." This added to the already existing stigma of having mental-health issues.

It caused me to ask, "What's wrong with me?" or have accusatory thoughts like, *Where is your faith? Why are your prayers not answered?* This would only compound the guilt and shame I was experiencing, because I thought, *I can't reach the level of faith of these people whom I love and admire. Why?*

Thank God, this has changed over the years. Medical science, increased knowledge, and wisdom in the Christian community have allowed us to realize that mental health is much more than a matter of faith. Ironically, come to find out, some of these same wonderful leaders and some of their family members also struggled with depression, but they did not have the freedom to talk about it. *That is why we are having this conversation.*

The conventional Christian view holds that we are a spirit, we have a soul, and we live in a physical body. When we are born again by believing that Jesus Christ is the Son of God and we accept the precious gift of salvation provided by His death, burial, and resurrection, our *spirit* is made alive unto God—pure, sacred, and holy. However, our souls and bodies are not born again. Our soul—which consists of our mind, will, emotions, imaginations, and attitudes—needs to be changed through a process referred to in the Bible as "the renewing of the mind." (See Romans 12:2.) Similarly, our body is unchanged at the new birth. It may have weaknesses, such as chemical imbalances, that need to be dealt with and healed.

As the psalmist David stated, we are "fearfully and wonderfully made" (Ps. 139:14). Each of us is incredibly unique, and *only* our Creator truly understands our individual makeup. Because we are a triune being, depression needs to be investigated on all three levels—spirit, soul, and body—and we need to incorporate all the knowledge we have gained throughout the centuries in dealing with it. (All knowledge comes from our loving heavenly Father.)

Let's look at epilepsy, for example. Precious people with this disease have seizures that come at times they can't control or understand. In the Bible, we see examples of people who were having seizures and were taken to Jesus. In each instance, He cast demons out of them. Now, although it may be true that depression and epilepsy can be caused by demonic activity, we have learned over the centuries that there is much more to these diseases than spiritual influence. Thankfully, medical science has done much to help epileptics through the discovery of various medications and processes that deal with the soul and the body to help eliminate seizures. The same is true for depression and mental-health issues.

Because we humans are such complex beings, we must deal with all the factors that contribute to depression in order to overcome it—spiritually, in our soul, and physically. Spiritually, is demonic oppression or influence an issue? Soulishly, what is going on in our thought life? Physically, is there a chemical imbalance in the body that is disrupting our sense of well-being? Are we taking care of our bodies through proper nutrition and exercise? What is our history? Has there been abuse? Physical and/or mental trauma? Have we experienced military combat? What else is the Lord revealing to us that could be contributing to our problems? Thank God we are not alone in our search. Friends, family members, doctors, nutritionists, ministers, psychologists, and psychiatrists can be a great help in our journey of discovery.

In this book, we will look at all these areas, each of which has helped me defeat depression. Remember, I am not a theologian, physician, or professional expert in these areas. The only thing that qualifies me to even write this book is that I have dealt with depression for many years. I am simply your friend who cares about you and wants to help ease your pain.

For you and me, this spells H-O-P-E.

Chapter 4

DEFEATING DEPRESSION ON A SPIRITUAL LEVEL

SINCE THE SPIRITUAL WORLD IS THE foundation of the natural world, we will first examine how depression can be dealt with in the spiritual arena.

The Miraculous

I believe in miracles. As I have mentioned, my spiritual father was Oral Roberts, who had a tremendous healing ministry and saw many miracles of every kind. I would certainly imagine there were supernatural healings of people with depression through his ministry.

However, his oldest son, Ronnie, suffered with depression and eventually committed suicide. How very tragic.

Yes, I believe that faith, the Holy Spirit, and God's Word can heal us of depression. I have prayed, stood on God's promises, believed Jesus "took my pain" on the cross, confessed healing Scriptures, and have had healing prayers prayed over me. I believe each of these things have helped me get through various episodes, but nothing has completely taken depression away. I don't know why.

One Bible teacher declares that it is unbelief that keeps us from experiencing healing. He believes that if we truly reach the state of "faith" with no doubt, the healing will come, regardless of what ails us. He quotes the Bible story from Mark 9:17–27 of a man whose son was mute and suffering convulsions.

When the father brought his son to the Healer, Jesus told the man, "If you can believe, all things are possible to him who believes" (v. 23).

To this, the man replied in tears, "Lord, I believe; help my unbelief!" (v. 24).

That has been my prayer many times, "Lord, I believe. Help my unbelief!" Jesus cast a demon out of the son, who was then completely healed. Although depression in my life has not been completely cured, I have *not* given up on faith, even if the black dog keeps returning.

The Power of Worship

You will show me the path of life;
In Your presence is fullness of joy;
At Your right hand are pleasures forevermore.
Psalm 16:11

Depression is not a new phenomenon. From their writings, we see that many Bible characters struggled with depression, David being my favorite. It appears that he dealt with depression by worshipping, crying out to God, and praising Him. There were times where David wept until he had no more tears, times where he felt totally forsaken, times he was paralyzed by the wave of depression that would come over him. There were times when he suffered from insomnia all night long and made his bed to swim with tears. (See Psalm 6:6.) In Psalm 55:5, fearfulness and trembling came upon him, which sounds like a panic attack to me. In Psalm 22:6, he said he felt like a worm, a disgrace, and worthless. (Self-hatred is another issue.) Psalm 13 describes the agony in his heart.

Still, David always knew how to "encourage himself in the Lord." (See 1 Samuel 30:1–6.) I believe one of the keys to encouraging himself was simply admitting his problem, crying out to God for help, and bringing God's presence upon himself through worship, music, and songs to God. Notice that I said, "*to* God." Psalm 22:3 says that God inhabits the praises of His people. When we sing *to* God, His presence invades the atmosphere!

The presence of God is real, tangible, and can be experienced on a spiritual, emotional, and even physical level. Of course, God is omnipresent, which means He is always present everywhere. However, I am talking about *experiencing* His presence, which is a bit of a mystery. What I am talking about is when God manifests Himself in a way that is so powerful, so precious, so real that you can actually *feel* it.

This is what the psalmist was referring to when he said, "In Your presence is fullness of joy; at Your right hand are pleasures forevermore" (Ps. 16:11). I have experienced this many times, and you can too! This experience is not dependent upon circumstances. In fact, I have experienced it *despite* my circumstances. I have wept, laughed, danced, literally felt "high," and experienced the most amazing love and peace when God's presence comes. This is what I want for you; and it is available right at this very moment, if you will but turn your thoughts to Him and express your love, admiration, and praise.

As a young adult, I was a part of a recording/publishing company with a few wonderful people. We had a dream of making records that would build God's kingdom. We called it Castle Records. We worked with some of the most talented and anointed artists, songwriters, and musicians of that day. Since we were following the Jesus Movement, our songs were mostly about Jesus and His Word. These songs were written *to people* (in contrast to being written *to God,* which I will explain later).

For several years, we worked incredibly hard to make a viable business, but we never had a breakthrough from a marketing/distribution standpoint. Finally, the "writing was on the wall." We were bankrupt. Although this was a profound disappointment for all of us, it threw me into a horrible episode of depression. I was devastated. Not knowing what to do, I went to the basement of the music studio and fell on my face. I stayed there a long time and felt like never getting up again. This went on every day for a few days, until a very strange thing happened—the presence of God came upon me.

I did not see a vision of Jesus or even hear His voice, but what I heard inside my heart was, "Ben, you have been helping others and promoting them, but I am calling *you* to lead people into my presence with your songs and encouragement. I want you to become a worshipper."

It was then that my paradigm shifted, and I began to write and sing songs that ministered *to* the Lord directly, instead of just *about* Him. As I did this, heaviness lifted, His presence would come, and a wonderful peace would wash over me. This experience was a foretaste of what God wanted to do for others through my music.

This reminds me of the biblical story where David played his harp as King Saul experienced depression from an evil spirit. As David played, the evil spirit would leave and King Saul's peace would be restored. (See 1 Samuel 16:14–23.) If depression is being caused by an evil spirit (and it can be), believe me, that evil spirit will leave us, too, when we worship Jesus and His presence "comes." I have experienced this many times and have received many testimonies from others who have been helped in this manner through my songs.

If you are dealing with depression, my first recommendation is that you become a worshipper of Jesus. Find content from anointed singers, musicians, preachers, teachers, and intercessors. Allow them to lead you into God's presence, where there is fullness of joy indeed. And, as Hebrews 13:15 tells us, "Let us continually offer the sacrifice of praise to God, that is, the fruit of our lips, giving thanks to His name."

There is tremendous power in having an attitude of gratitude. It will do much to keep the black dog at bay. It affects the macro world, the quantum world, and even our bodies and our brains down to a cellular level.[2] It is an amazing fact that even our brain cells react positively when we are grateful.[3] I am constantly giving thanks to God for His goodness, even for the small, seemingly insignificant things, because all good comes from God. (See James 1:17.) Having a grateful heart helps me so much that I could write an entire book about it.

God's Word

There is power, life, and healing in God's Word. His Word can bring His presence. In fact, during the last episode of depression I suffered, I believe I received a revelation that helped me get through it. I believe it can help you too.

Second Timothy 1:7 states, "God has not given us a spirit of fear, but of power and of love and of a sound mind." Thank God, a spirit of fear has not been given to us by God, but He *has given us* the spirit of power, love, and a *sound mind*. We should be so grateful for these gifts—and we should absolutely believe that God has given them to us!

Jesus said, "I have come that they may have life, and that they may have it more abundantly" (John 10:10). This abundant life is another gift to be thankful for. In the same verse, Jesus also said, "The thief (Satan) does not come except to steal, and to kill, and to destroy."

So, I said, "Wait a minute! If God gave me a sound mind and Satan comes (through depression, anxiety, and panic) to steal my sound mind, I've got something to say about this!"

I remember my mom and dad gave me a football for Christmas when I was about seven years old. It was a gift that I cherished, so much so that I even slept with it! I loved that football so much that I wasn't going to allow anyone to take it from me, not even my own two brothers. If anyone did try to take it (and there were times they did), I was willing to fight for it.

With this in mind during the episode of depression that I have been describing, I said to myself, *Alright then, I am going to fight to keep anyone, including the devil, from taking my sound mind, just like I was willing to fight to keep my football.* I took a strong stand and said aloud, "No, Mr. Devil! You can't have my sound mind!" Guess what, in just a few days, I came out of that depression and was restored to my sound mind! The next time you start experiencing depression, I encourage you to take a stand and fight the good fight of faith. I am cheering you on, and you will win!

The Bible is literally full of Scriptures that state God's promises and enable and comfort us in times of trouble. I recommend that you and I stay close to the Bible. It is our best friend when the storm of depression comes.

I read a recent study that really troubled me. It indicated that only nine percent of professing Christians read their Bibles every day. This is tragic, because God's Word feeds and strengthens our spirit and builds our faith. *Not* reading the Bible every day can certainly leave the gate open for the black dog to attack.

Jesus Suffered Depression for You and Me

As I have described before, depression can be summed up as *utter hopelessness*, *profound insecurity*, and a *feeling of desperation* stemming from a false reality that says all is coming to a terrible end. As a result of these "feelings," the brain generates pain that is unbearable, insufferable. If you have experienced depression, you will understand what these words mean. If you have a loved one who is experiencing depression, this is what he or she is dealing with.

As Christians, we believe that Jesus is the Son of God and that He was with God in the beginning. (See John

1:1–2.) He literally lived an eternal existence as one with the Father God Almighty. Think about how glorious this life must have been. Together, they created the wonderful world we live in, all the plants, animals, geography, topography, and geology. It all came from the heart of God in union with His Son, Jesus. All the various and glorious expressions of the human race also came from their unlimited creativity. It is hard to imagine the eternal joy, peace, glory, and excitement that must have been involved in this relationship. Most of all, imagine the total and complete love they had for one another! Wow, what a union!

Before the foundations of the earth, God—in His infinite wisdom—devised a plan: He would send His Son to Earth to pay the penalty for the sin human beings would fall into and redeem them from the resulting curse. Jesus came in obedience to this epic plan of redemption, which was conceived in the Father's heart. He showed us the love of the Father, the character of the Father, and the intentions of the Father to completely reconcile mankind to our original relationship of oneness with Him.

The only way this could be accomplished was for Jesus to lay down His life as punishment for the sins of the world, to take on our iniquities, bear our sorrows, and carry our pains. (See Isaiah 53:4–5 and Matthew

8:17.) For Jesus to take sin upon Himself, it would separate Him from His Father for the first (and only) time in eternity.

Let's look at Jesus as He suffered this punishment on the cross. "About the ninth hour (3 p.m.) Jesus cried out with a loud voice, saying, '… MY GOD, MY GOD, WHY HAVE YOU FORSAKEN ME?'" (Mt. 27:46). This was a true statement, as sin did indeed cause a holy God to forsake His only Son. Think about the emotional pain this must have brought upon Jesus to go from having an eternal relationship with a loving Father to *nothing!* His God and Father *gone!* How insecure, how hopeless, how foreign and strange this must have felt to Jesus. No doubt He experienced utter hopelessness, profound insecurity, and a feeling of desperation from a (false) reality that all was coming to a terrible end.

Well, dear friend, Jesus did this for us, for *you!* He *bore* our depression on the cross, and by the lashes laid upon His back (the Bible calls them "stripes"), we were healed. This was done so that we might die to sin and be restored to relationship with our Father. (See 1 Peter 2:24.) Therefore, I believe the highest and most ideal way we can be healed is to receive this truth.

We need to take time—as long as it takes—to meditate on this reality until it goes from a mere mental thought to a deep revelation in our spirits. It must really "dawn on" us that Jesus bore our pain of depression. When this takes place, we can come to a place where we truly let our depression, mental pain, and anguish *go* to the cross, where it belongs! When we truly see our depression being taken and suffered by Jesus on the cross, it will leave us. This is the power of faith. "All things are possible to him who believes" (Mark 9:23).

Take time to get quiet, pull out these Scriptures, and use your imagination to see the misery Jesus was going through when He was forsaken by His Father. Identify this pain with the pain that you are experiencing from depression, and say, "Jesus, I release this pain in my mind and my soul to You. I connect with your gift of love in bearing my pain on the cross, and I receive my healing from depression—*now!*"

Many may never get to this place of healing, because they do not take the time to focus on Jesus bearing their pain and sickness. Meditation takes time and patience, but it is how truth *impacts* our natural reality. Many of us are like people digging for gold. Even if we know the gold is there, we dig a little here and a little there, but we are continually disappointed by not finding it! But if we will make the effort and be determined to dig deeper, deeper, and deeper still, eventually, we will strike gold. This is what we must do with God's Word. I want to press in until this great exchange takes place in my own life, where depression truly *goes* to the cross and *away* from me! I invite you to join me in this spiritual aspect of our journey toward freedom. We can get there!

You may say, "I'm sorry, but I'm just not there." That's OK. Thank God, Jesus understands our depression and where we are; He experienced every pain that we do. Please do not feel ashamed or condemned. God certainly doesn't condemn or criticize you. Receiving healing through spiritual means is only one way that God has provided for us to receive relief from depression. As we continue, we will explore many other ways that can help.

More on Meditation

Many other religions, mind-science practitioners, neuroscientists, mystics, and millions of others have discovered the power of meditation. Though they have discovered and used meditation for great benefit, I believe it is the Father of our Lord Jesus Christ, the Creator of all things, who created us with this spirit/mind/body connection.

Take electricity, for example. Though Benjamin Franklin may have discovered it, he didn't invent it. It was actually created and put on the planet by our heavenly

Father. Although people from all walks of life, all beliefs, and religions can use electricity for great benefit, it is a gift put here for us to discover by our Creator, the Father of our Lord Jesus Christ. Similarly, this is true regarding meditation.

Here is why I believe this. The book of Joshua in the Bible was estimated to have been written between 1400 and 1370 B.C., long before neuroscience was discovered. The first chapter of Joshua says in verse 8:

This Book of the Law shall not depart from your mouth, but you shall meditate in it day and night, that you may observe to do according to all that is written in it. For then you will make your way prosperous, and then you will have good success.

Wow! This is an amazing promise. The Hebrew word for "prosperous" includes the Jewish concept of *shalom*, which means perfect peace, contentment, and prosperity—complete wholeness.[4] Certainly, this includes mental-health benefits!

Christian leaders sometimes mention meditation, but I wish they would teach people more specifically *how* to meditate. Leaders of alternate religions, neuroscientists, mystics, and others teach people the art and practice of meditation and obtain great, even miraculous, results. It just doesn't make sense to me that more Christian leaders don't offer guidance in this area since it was invented by our heavenly Father. *He* commanded us to do it day and night, so we could prosper, have good success, and live in peace.

Cecilie Croissant, a wonderful Christian counselor, says in her book, *Enjoying the Journey of Transformation,* "Biblical meditation is the greatest thing ever, because it causes the Scripture to become alive to us and a part of us."[5] To me, it doesn't matter how you learn the art of meditation, as long as we can develop this powerful practice to meditate on God's Word and biblical principles. This is what I have done with good results. I want to share with you my very layman's lesson on how to meditate. I believe this will help you. Do it especially if you are experiencing depression, anxiety, or panic. I invite you to listen to the guided meditation I created for you on my YouTube channel.[6]

bencares.com

First, find a portion of Scripture that you want to come alive to you. Let's use the verse that I shared with you earlier, 2 Timothy 1:7. "God has not given us a spirit of fear, but of power and of love and of a sound mind." OK!

Now, block off some time. I recommend at least thirty minutes, which I realize might seem like a long time at first. If you do this like the Bible commands (day and night), you will become good at it and be able to meditate for longer periods of time after a while. Don't be surprised if at first your mind and body fight you. This is normal. When I first started, I thought, *Man, I can't stand this! How do I stay still for thirty minutes?* I thought I was coming unglued, but I pressed through.

Next, turn off or put aside all media, phones, televisions, computers, etc. Find a quiet spot where you can be alone, uninterrupted. Find a comfortable place to sit up or lie down. *Relax!*

Then, become aware of your breathing. Focused breathing fills your brain and body with oxygen, which feeds all the cells down to the quantum level. Breathe slowly and deeply at least thirty times, letting go of everything that is on your mind. Do it again. Then, do it again. Yes, at least ninety deep breaths. Completely relax all your muscles and nerves. If you are especially tight in an area, it may help to focus on that area, then let go as you breathe out. In the quiet, begin to feel gratitude—literally count your blessings.

Now, begin thinking about the Scripture you want to internalize. Pray and ask the Holy Spirit to reveal this Word to your spirit, soul, and body. He will.

One definition of the word *meditate* is "to mutter." Slowly and repeatedly, think about the verse and say it—first in your mind, then speak it out of your mouth, over and over: "God has given me a spirit of power, love, and a sound mind." Now, focus on your body and cause it to literally feel the truth of those words. Go over it again and again, and soon you will literally *feel* the power, the peace, the truth.

Once you get to this point, mentally change your internal stance to that of a warrior, one who fights. With this in mind, say out loud emphatically, "God has given me a sound mind! Nothing, no one, no circumstance is going to take this gift away from me!"

Matthew 11:12 says, "The kingdom of heaven suffers violence, and the violent take it by force." Give thanks and praise to God for your sound mind! Be like I was as a little kid with my football! Take hold of that promise and refuse to let go!

Be patient with yourself; meditation is not easy at first. However, when you regularly (day and night) meditate on God's Word, don't be surprised when the black dog becomes quiet, whimpers, and takes off, leaving you with your sound mind!

John 1:14 says, "The Word became flesh and dwelt among us." As you meditate on God's Word, it will literally become part of your flesh. Neuroscientists suggest that meditation can actually affect your body on a cellular level, completely change your chemistry, and even influence your DNA.[7] Wow!

The Power of Imagination

Using your imagination, or visualization, is done in conjunction with and as a part of meditation. After you meditate on the Words of God, use your imagination to begin *creating a powerful vision of the future as you want it to be, depression free!* Develop the art of seeing yourself as a happy, joyful, peaceful person. Focus on it until you can almost taste it. As you visualize this picture of yourself consistently over time, the spiritual law says that you will become what you imagine. "For as he thinks in his heart, so is he" (Prov. 23:7).

Victor Frankl was a neurologist, psychiatrist, philosopher, and prisoner of war during World War II.

He survived the Holocaust and the Nazi concentration camps. After his ordeal, he wrote a book about his experience entitled, *Man's Search for Meaning.* Dr. Frankl observed his fellow prisoners of war over time. He saw many die and witnessed some, like himself, who survived.

He concluded that the main factor of those who survived was that they developed a strong vision of "seeing themselves being out of the prison." On the other hand, he also stated that those who put a date on their vision of freedom continued to be disappointed as each "deadline" passed. Sadly, many of these individuals died. For instance, if they said, "We will be free by Christmas," they were profoundly disappointed when it didn't come to pass in their time frame, and some perished. On the contrary, those who developed a vision and resolve that they *would* survive—regardless of how long it took— were more likely to make it through, no matter how difficult it was.

I believe this is true in defeating depression. If we, through meditating on God's Word, can *see* ourselves free of depression, and we are resolved that we will get through it no matter what or how long it takes, we have a better chance of overcoming each episode and eventually become totally free.

The Beauty of God's Grace and Goodness

They say hindsight is perfect. As I look back on the battles that I have had with mental health, one thing I know for sure, and I want to repeat, it has been the wonderful grace of my loving heavenly Father that literally carried me through. And it is carrying you now! God's grace is stronger, mightier than any issue we can ever face. It may not feel like it at this time, but His *grace* is carrying you even when you feel like death is at the door. Oh, how wonderful is the grace of God! As the lyrics of the song, "Amazing Grace," so accurately proclaim, "'Tis grace that brought me safe thus far and grace will lead me home." Trust in God's grace, trust in His goodness, trust in His faithfulness, and you will prevail.

Taking Communion

Jesus' body was broken for us. He bore our sorrows. When we take Communion, we remember anew His agony, His mental and emotional pain. Yes, *He* suffered depression on the cross. Yes, He is acquainted with our grief. Yes, He suffered the punishment required for our peace. (See Isaiah 53:4–5.) See this, feel it, be grateful for it.

Sometimes people try to portray God and the devil as opponents of equal status in the same boxing ring.

How ridiculous! First of all, God is Creator of all things and He created the devil. (God created the devil as a magnificent angel, who later rebelled against God. See Ezekiel 28:12–19 and Isaiah 14:12.) Secondly, God is complete goodness. In Ephesians 3, the apostle Paul prays for us to have a revelation of—to really come to know on an experiential level—God's love. His love and goodness are *infinitely* greater, bigger, and far more consuming than anything bad the world, the flesh, or the devil can throw at us. Praise God!

The Holy Spirit as Counselor

Thank God we have the greatest Counselor on Earth, if we have received Christ. This Counselor is the Holy Spirit. It's easy to think that if we just had Jesus in the flesh, all of our problems would cease; however, Jesus said it was actually good that He go away, because He would send us the Holy Spirit. (See John 14:15–27.) Jesus knew the disciples would be troubled with His talk of going away, but I love His compassion toward them when He said, "Let not your heart be troubled, neither let it be afraid" (v. 27). I love how Jesus was always thoughtful toward what His disciples were feeling.

Notice verses 16 and 17 from the *Amplified Bible* (I like this translation because it amplifies, or expounds upon, the words from the original Greek text): Jesus said, "I will ask the Father, and He will give you another Comforter (Counselor, Helper, Intercessor, Advocate, Strengthener, and Standby), that He may remain with you forever—the Spirit of Truth." Knowing the truth is what sets us free. (See John 8:32.)

Although I have had help from counselors over the years, I recently had a wonderful experience with the Holy Spirit that I want to share with you. During a three-day holiday weekend, I decided to go to Kansas City and spend three days in the International House of Prayer 24/7 Prayer Room. The first day, I enjoyed a beautiful time of prayer, worship, and experiencing the praise music and atmosphere of intercession that they have created in the prayer room. Nothing really dramatic happened, but I enjoyed lifting up my family, friends, and future to God in prayer.

The second morning was much the same. I prayed until lunchtime, then went to get something to eat. After lunch, there was a special young lady leading worship. I sensed a strong anointing, and I was enjoying entering into God's presence as she led the songs. After about thirty minutes, all of a sudden, "something" came upon me! I started weeping—tears flowed from the depths of my being and I felt like I was literally being shaken. I couldn't stop. This was totally unexpected, and I promise I didn't just conjure it up.

My face became wet from tears. I was undone, messed up. I knew something was happening in my soul, so I asked the Lord, "What is this?" At that moment, I knew it was the Holy Spirit visiting me to heal a deep hurt that had come from rejection and betrayal fifteen years before! I had forgiven, released the person to God, and gone on with my life; but for some reason, I just couldn't get over the hurt. It was like I was carrying it but couldn't get it resolved. I had prayed many times, sought human counseling, had others pray over me, but I couldn't get over it—till now.

So, I continued to weep and shake on my knees for another hour or so. The whole episode took about two hours and half a box of tissue. However, when I stood up and collected myself, that deep pain was *totally gone! Hallelujah!* The great Counselor had prevailed!

Certainly, I thank God for all the people who are called to study and practice counseling and therapy as a vocation. In the next chapter, we will discuss some of the help I have received from them. God definitely uses people to bring healing from these wounds. But remember, despite their best intentions, they will even admit that they are "practicing" and don't always get it right. The Holy Spirit is the Spirit of Truth. He always gets it right.

As we have read, there are a variety of things we can do from a spiritual standpoint to combat depression. Next, we will take a look at tools from a soulish, or psychological, perspective.

Chapter 5

~

DEALING WITH DEPRESSION ON A PSYCHOLOGICAL LEVEL

ALL OF THE SPIRITUAL TOOLS CAN be a great help to us; however, sometimes we need the help of a mental-health professional—a licensed, professional counselor or psychologist. There is no shame in needing help from an outside source; we all need assistance at times.

Many of us who experience depression have wounds deep in our souls that we don't know how to deal with. These come from incidents of abuse, trauma, rejection, abandonment, and other situations. These are hurts that have yet to be healed and continue to torment us. They can throw us into an episode of depression, if we are so inclined. Many times, a skilled counselor or psychologist can help identify these injuries and offer tools that will bring healing and recovery.

I encourage you to find a gifted, Bible-believing, Spirit-filled Christian professional who will bring God's Word and the best therapy techniques to bear in your counseling sessions. Please steer clear of those who practice from a simply scientific basis and don't invite the Holy Spirit to take part. I thank God for all the discoveries that have been made in psychological counseling, but it is important that one combines the science with the spiritual principles of God's Word in his or her practice. I have listed some references in the back of this book for your convenience.

There are several types of counseling techniques used by counselors and psychologists. Some of these include neurofeedback and EMDR (which is especially helpful in healing damage from traumatic events).

Neurofeedback

Neurofeedback is a treatment option available to treat anxiety, depression, PTSD, ADHD, sleep disorders, and a host of other psychological issues. It is non-invasive, medication free, and encourages the brain to develop healthier patterns of activity. According to Dr. Suruchi Chandra, "The goal of treatment is not only to change how you think and feel, but also to change your brain on a biological level for better functioning."[8]

If our brain waves are too slow or too fast, we may feel tired or too keyed up. Harmonized brain waves are essential for our brains to function optimally as God designed and for us to feel a sense of well-being and balance. Anna Raab, MA, BCN, of Abundant Living Neurofeedback and Counseling states, "With neurofeedback, we will measure your brain's electrical patterns through qEEG Brain Mapping and train your brain wave patterns to normalize. As your brain waves normalize, symptoms dissolve and true healing occurs."[9] The following is a testimonial from one of her clients:

> I was severely depressed. I had no motivation or energy to do anything. I was tired all the time and did not have much will for anything. I was melancholy, isolated, and lonely.
>
> My relationship with my husband was deteriorating and full of tension, hurt, misunderstanding, and no communication. We were on the brink of divorce. It was either this [neurofeedback] or divorce.

Now I'm so much better. I cannot even bring myself into a depressed state—even when I revisit thoughts I used to have. It's amazing. I no longer feel like something is slowly killing me. I just wanted to be gone. It's like somebody plugged me back in. I have energy, motivation, and the will to live.

My husband says I'm motivated, confident, and assertive. And where communicating wasn't even possible before, we are now well on our way to working out our issues. I'm doing a million times better.[10]

There are many articles available online to explain the process of neurofeedback and how it works. Suffice it to say here that many have experienced tremendous breakthroughs as their brain waves are brought into balance.

EMDR

Sometimes depression is a result of experiencing trauma. An effective therapy technique used by many therapists to treat this is Eye Movement Desensitization Reprocessing, or EMDR. According to Cecilie Croissant, MA, LPC, and an approved EMDR consultant:

EMDR is a structured therapy that helps people recover from trauma and PTSD symptoms. When a patient focuses briefly on the traumatic incident while simultaneously experiencing bilateral stimulation (e.g. eye movements side to side), the emotion and vividness of the trauma are reduced.

As an EMDR therapist, I have been amazed at how speedily people can process through tragic or horrific events and come to a place of peace and neutrality about them. The memories are still there, but the fight, flight, or freeze responses are gone.

Most of us have experienced what I call trauma with a small *t*. One of my clients remembered often feeling left out among classmates. At the same time, she experienced shame due to frequent criticism and lack of encouragement at home. Repeated incidents caused her to develop certain beliefs about herself. Later, as a teen and an adult, she acted in ways that reinforced those beliefs, and she ended up with anxiety and depression. Treating the memories through EMDR helped this woman to "connect the dots" of her experience as well as embrace adaptive and more truthful and accurate beliefs about herself.

This in turn changed her outlook, and her life started improving in several areas.

With more acute traumatic situations, such as sexual assault, childhood abuse, witnessing violence, or serious car accidents, EMDR helps the brain process the memories on a neurological level, which leads to a cognitive shift. Triggers are neutralized, and the individual regains a sense of control in their lives. As a Christian believer and therapist, I feel fortunate to be a part of seeing people find healing and wholeness through this wonderful tool.

Interestingly, even the U.S. Department of Veteran's Affairs recommends EMDR as a treatment for PTSD. A simple Google search will take you to their website.[11]

Chapter 6

~

DEALING WITH DEPRESSION ON A PHYSICAL LEVEL

WE CAN ALSO DEAL WITH DEPRESSION on a physical level. Diet, nutrition, and exercise are all vital elements that can help us climb out of the depression "hole."

Medical Doctors

As we have stated, depression is many faceted, and it sometimes has a physiological component. I am grateful for the discoveries in neuroscience that have greatly helped people deal with depression. Your primary care physician may be a good place to start, and there are also psychiatrists, who are medical specialists specifically trained to determine if a chemical imbalance may be causing the problem. As I was growing up, there was a stigma about going to a "shrink," and this caused many people to shy away from going to these specialists. Thankfully, much progress has been made concerning mental-health issues coming to the surface in our culture. Today we can receive this type of help without shame or fear.

A chemical imbalance can be likened to a vitamin deficiency. If a doctor discovers that we are lacking in a certain vitamin—Vitamin C, for example—he may suggest taking Vitamin C supplements to correct the problem. Of course, there is nothing wrong with that; it is completely acceptable. It is much the same with a chemical imbalance. There are four primary chemicals that can drive the positive emotions you should feel each day: dopamine, oxytocin, serotonin, and endorphins.

Dopamine is a chemical that gives you a happy feeling when someone likes your post on Instagram, when you get a good message on FB or a text, a positive phone call, or when completing a task. It is a primary source of an overall sense of well-being and motivation. Dopamine deficiency symptoms include low self-esteem, procrastination, lack of motivation, fatigue, feeling anxious, and feeling hopeless, to name a few.[12]

Oxytocin is the chemical that is released by the brain during physical contact with others, such as a handshake, hug, or pat on the back. It causes the feeling behind love, friendship, or deep trust. It boosts our immune system, makes us better problem solvers, and gives us lasting feelings of calm and safety. Oxytocin deficiency symptoms include insomnia, having low energy, feeling lonely, stressed, or disconnected from relationships.[13]

Serotonin is also a social chemical. When we feel a sense of accomplishment or recognition from others, we are experiencing the effects of serotonin. It can come from graduating from school, finishing a race, or being appreciated for hard work. Serotonin can create strong, positive emotions. A deficiency in this neurotransmitter includes symptoms of anxiety or panic attacks, depression, hopelessness, social phobias, compulsive disorders, and insomnia.[14]

Endorphins are powerful chemicals. I used to be a recreational runner and experienced the effects of a "runner's high," which takes place as a person's body expends its energy and endorphins are released. Fundamentally, endorphins are released in our bodies as a response to pain, once we press past our comfort level. Doctors tell us that we all need three to four big belly laughs each day, because this is another way the body releases endorphins. These, in turn, raise our level of happiness. It is imperative for us to exercise when dealing with depression. Endorphin deficiency symptoms include bodily aches and pains, impulsive behavior, anxiety, depression, mood swings, and insomnia.[15]

It is truly amazing that our bodies produce these chemicals from the foods we eat, the air we breathe, and the processes of our physical bodies. For instance, most of the serotonin and other "feel good" chemicals are manufactured in the digestive tract (small and large intestines). They are then fed to the brain through the circulatory system. Finally, the brain releases them from the intelligence it receives as a result of what the body is going through and needs.[16] Indeed, we are fearfully and wonderfully made!

As with vitamins in our bodies, sometimes our bodily chemicals become imbalanced and cause us to feel anxious, depressed, hopeless, etc. If so, doctors are trained to diagnose and treat these ailments. Some of the treatments they prescribe may include:

- Exercise—increasing daily activity

- Herbal supplements

- Antidepressants

- Dietary balance

- Counseling to help face traumatic, life-altering events

- Cognitive behavioral therapy

- Support network—contact with people

- Meditation

- Acupuncture

Nutritionists

Our brains are part of our bodies, so it stands to reason that anything that makes our bodies healthier will also make our brains healthier. These things include fresh air, sunshine, clean water, exercise, de-stressing, vitamins and minerals, and improved circulation, to name a few.

The following are some of the nutrients particularly linked to brain health.

- **Omega-3 fatty acids:** These nutrients are found in fish, nuts, seeds, and algae oil. Omega-3 fatty acids provide building blocks for healthy brain development. These literally "lubricate" the brain and promote normal function. This is why they are recommended for their potential role in helping deal with depression.

- **B vitamins:** This is referred to as "the happy vitamin." These nutrients are found in meat, eggs, seafood, green leafy vegetables, legumes, and whole grains. Studies have shown that a deficiency in B vitamins (particularly B-12) can be linked to depression. According to a 2014 study from the *British Journal of Psychiatry,* supplementing with B-12, B-6, and folic acid improved subjects' response to antidepressant medications.[17]

- **Vitamin D:** This nutrient is found in sun exposure and fortified breakfast cereals, breads, juices, and milk. Vitamin D is required for brain development and function. Deficiency in this "sunshine vitamin" is sometimes associated with depression and other mood disorders; however, having plenty of this vitamin may improve happiness.

- **Selenium:** This nutrient is found in cod, Brazil nuts, walnuts, and poultry. Selenium is an essential mineral, meaning we have to obtain it from food. Among its various roles, selenium works with other nutrients to create antioxidant balance in our body's cells. Many studies have shown a link between low selenium and depression. One hypothesis is that selenium's function as an antioxidant could be necessary for preventing or managing depression.

- **Tryptophan:** This nutrient is found in protein sources including turkey, beef, eggs, some dairy products, and dark leafy greens. An amino acid, tryptophan is a precursor to serotonin. It's not well understood, but low tryptophan seems to trigger depressive symptoms in some people who have taken antidepressants.

I have shared some things that will benefit you, but I would be remiss if I did not also include some things that can add to your problem instead of solving it. It is easy to look to some of these for comfort, but the more you can avoid them, the better you will deal with depression.

Things to Avoid

- **Alcohol** is a nervous-system depressant. It might give a little relief in the short term, but it is definitely a downer.

- **Caffeine** brings you up then knocks you down. It may also worsen anxiety and insomnia.

- **Sugar** may numb the pain or distract you from it for a while, but eventually it makes you feel worse emotionally and physically, especially since it can worsen inflammation. You may have heard of the "sugar blues." Add this to real depression and the problem is compounded.

- **Processed foods** can also make you feel worse. Some folks notice that they are sensitive to things like preservatives or chemicals in these foods.[18]

Earlier I shared about a doctor I met in Santa Fe. He was extremely concerned about the chemicals we put in our food, air, lawns, water, and bodies. He believed that many of the diseases we deal with are brought on by all the chemicals, hormones, and processes in our society. For instance, he was deeply worried about all the sugar we consume in our foods and believed diabetes could one day bankrupt our country.

Turns out, just plain ole, good clean living, eating, and drinking will certainly make a big difference. Come on, we can do it!

Before we proceed, let me say a word about motivation. I understand that when you are in a negative psychological state, it is especially difficult to discipline yourself in these areas. After all, one of the terrible symptoms of depression is a lack of motivation, an almost paralyzing state of mind. It is so hard to eat right, to exercise, and to refrain from harmful foods, drinks, or drugs. Believe me, I get it. As your friend, however, I feel I must give you a gentle "kick in the rear" to encourage you to take the right steps. Finding a trusted health professional such as a registered dietician or nutritionist can be a great support in helping you overcome the motivation problem. If you don't feel like you can make major changes all at once, that's understandable and it's OK. Just start small and work your way up. You don't have to take giant steps. Baby steps can lead you to your destination of wholeness.

Exercise

This is an area that is particularly difficult when you're depressed and unmotivated, because your world shrinks to a tiny little black hole when you are fighting the black dog. But it is one thing that has been proven to help. In my own life, one of the things that helped me so much was running. Though not competitive, I ran about a thousand miles a year for over twenty years. This was probably one of the main factors in the physical arena that helped me deal with depression. When you run, walk, or swim, your cardiovascular system is exercised, and oxygen is forced into the cells, causing endorphins to be released. Remember, endorphins are part of the "feel good" chemicals that our bodies produce.

During my running years, there were so many times that I would be depressed and found it next to impossible to muster up the strength to begin. But I learned to start the process by breaking it down into baby steps. First, I'd put on my running clothes. Then I would think, *Just take one step*. Then I'd take another, then another. I can't tell you how many times I did this to get myself started, but I can honestly say, I *never* regretted taking a run, no matter how difficult it was to discipline myself to do it.

After years of running, I switched to walking several times a week, which basically accomplishes the same thing. So, if you can't run, how about walking? One reason I enjoy walking so much these days is that I notice more of nature and beautiful scenery than when I ran. Plus, I also use my walking time to pray and commune with my Father. That's not so easy when running.

Because of my own experience and what so many health professionals have discovered, I highly recommend that you begin a consistent regimen of running, walking, or swimming, so oxygen can energize your mood and create a better outlook. If, for whatever reason, you are unable to take part in such activities, the following are some other suggestions:

- **Step outside and expose yourself to sunlight**. There's a reason depression is associated with darkness. Sunlight provides Vitamin D for a sense of well-being.

- **Ask for help**. Start to find your tribe of helpers. It may include a doctor, a therapist, close supportive friends and family members, a fitness trainer, even a pet.

- **Move**. Depression is immobilizing. Do your best to act against that force by moving whatever you can move, however you can move it. Our bodies were not created to sit or be immobile—we were created to *move!*

- **Express yourself**. Draw, write, talk about what you're feeling, howl at the moon, or beat up a punching bag. Do whatever pushes the bad stuff out. Don't keep it all inside.

As I mentioned, I understand that motivating yourself to do any of these things is especially challenging when you are in the midst of depression or other mental-health difficulties. I encourage you to focus on the results that each of these suggestions promise. Start small. Do something constructive to help yourself. I promise, it gets easier.

Chapter 7

⁓

SUMMARY AND
MY BEST ADVICE

IN CLOSING, I WANT TO SHARE with you my best advice for helping you to live a productive, happy, and prosperous life, regardless of how low you may feel or how hopeless it seems at the moment.

Gratitude

Neuroscientists are now confirming the power of the many scriptural admonitions to "give thanks always." Even if you feel like the whole world is caving in on you, there is always much to be thankful for. *Every* day, take a few minutes to put yourself in an attitude of gratitude. List and express the many things you are thankful for, even if it starts with being thankful for the breath in your lungs. Gratitude creates neuro- and spiritual pathways to receive grace and more grace. Many times at my lowest point, even when I would pull the covers over my head, I would start whispering, "Thank You God for my hair, my eyes, my ears, my heart, my lungs," going down my body, giving thanks for the smallest things. And soon I would feel relief.

Forgiveness

Does that word strike a nerve? We have all been wronged and hurt by people during our lifetimes; however, holding unforgiveness or bitterness is a sure path that will lead to depression, anxiety, and other mental troubles. Maybe things have happened to you that are unthinkable and seemingly unforgiveable. If so, I would like to walk through the process of forgiveness with you. I encourage you to find a quiet place, then picture the person or group that has hurt you and been unjust toward you. See the person(s) in your mind's eye.

Next, turn your attention to Jesus and imagine how brutalized, abused, and betrayed He was. The beating was so severe that He was unrecognizable as He hung on the cross. All this, yet He was innocent. In the midst of His torment, however, He uttered, "Father, forgive them, for they do not know what they do" (Luke 23:34).

Next, remember the many ways you have sinned or missed the mark during your lifetime. Realize how deep His forgiveness is toward you—He holds not one sin against you. If God can forgive you and lives in you, then you are capable of forgiving whatever has been done to you. Even if you don't *feel* it, you can make the decision to forgive and let the person go.

It's as simple as saying the following prayer: "Father, thank You for forgiving me my many trespasses and sins. I receive Your forgiveness. Now I choose to forgive _____. I release this person(s) from his/her offense, and I release myself from the unforgiveness that is hurting me. Thank You for it."

Saying a prayer like this aloud will bring about a peace that passes understanding and will allow your spirit, soul, and body to operate in harmony as God designed.

Talk to Yourself

No, you are not crazy if you talk to yourself. In fact, everybody talks to themselves! The question is, what are we saying? The truth is, we become what we tell ourselves. Proverbs 23:7 KJV says, "As he thinketh in his heart, so is he." The word *thinketh* can also be paraphrased as, "Whatever a man *tells himself*, so is he!"

One of the most brutal tactics of the evil kingdom is to get us to despise, hate, and condemn ourselves. (I've been there.) This is a direct route to an episode and ongoing attitude of depression. For years, I would blame myself anytime something bad happened. I'd literally "set myself up" for bad things to happen by my self-talk. This added to the already existing problem of depression I experienced.

My friend, the reason this is such a terrible thing to do is that it completely goes against the way God sees you or what God would say to you. God is love. Yes, sometimes love calls for correction and discipline, but if you think it is God that is condemning and rejecting you, you have not had a sufficient revelation of His love. Anytime you "hear a message" about yourself that is hateful, degrading, and mean, I can guarantee you, *it is not God's voice!* God's voice, even if it is for correction, will come to you in a gentle, loving way and tell you the truth. The truth is, you are the prized possession of a loving heavenly Father; and even though He knows your thoughts, sins, and bad attitudes, He looks past them at the precious treasure that He created—*you!* He will work to "lead you in the paths of righteousness," as the psalmist David said in Psalm 23. Jesus took our sins out of the way so that we could have this type of relationship with our heavenly Father.

We have already talked about how David evidently experienced depression many times in his life. However, let's look at his self-talk: Both Psalm 42:5, 11 and 43:5 say basically the same things: "Why are you cast down, O my soul? And why are you disquieted within me? Hope in God; for I shall yet praise Him, the help of my countenance and my God." Yes, David admitted that he was depressed, but as they say where I come from, "He gave himself a talkin' to." He encouraged himself in the Lord. The Scriptures contain many such examples.

I want to share one thing that I have done that really has helped me, and it is something that I recommend that you do. I have used my voice memo app on my phone to record some positive self-talk, and then I have played it to myself when I have gone to bed, when I have gotten up in the morning, and anytime I have felt down. I have used Scripture and quoted it to myself.

For example, "I am Ben Ferrell, I am a child of God. My heavenly Father loves me more than I can ever imagine. He carefully watches over me and takes care of me. His joy and His peace continually comfort me. His plan and purpose for my life are coming to pass, and I am continually giving thanks to Him throughout the day.

He meets my every need and demonstrates His love for me in many ways every day!"

I highly encourage you to take your favorite Scriptures and create some *awesome* self-talk for yourself, because the fact is—*you are awesome!*

Work

God created a need in humans to be productive, to create, to manage, to organize, and yes, to work! Work, done with the right attitude, can be a joyful and fulfilling experience. We are made to work and to enjoy our work. Even God, after He created things each day, looked over His creation and said, "It is good!" It brought Him joy to reflect on the results of His work. (See Genesis 1.)

In my opinion, it is a mistake to allow depression and mental health issues to stop us from working and being productive. In fact, being non-productive adds to our negative self-talk and depression. I know it is hard; and when you are depressed, the last thing you want to do is work because you have no motivation. But you can take baby steps to be productive and find some joy in work.

I remember one time when I was going through a terrible episode of depression. I actually wanted to go to bed, cover my head, and stay there. But I decided to take a baby step towards coming out of the pit. I went to my closet and started organizing my clothes. Pants, shirts, suits, coats, shoes—I lined them all up in a row, color coded them, and organized everything. It took awhile, but after I saw everything in order, I felt a joy and satisfaction that wouldn't have come if I had stayed in bed.

If you have a job, take pleasure in accomplishing the service or the tasks that you do. Focus on them, get them done one by one, look over your accomplishments and say, "It is good!" If you currently can't handle a full-time job, find work around the house—not too much as to overwhelm you, but simple tasks that can bring the joy of applying yourself to something and seeing the results. It will do so much for your mental health and attitude. Fight laziness with all your might; it will only add to your problem. Get busy! Even taking baby steps will lead you to a better place mentally.

Play

I remember one of the most successful ministers in the world made a statement to one of my friends. "If it would not have been for golf, I would have never made it." When I heard this, I thought, *How can that be? Here is a man of God who touched the whole world with the gospel and built a tremendous ministry and legacy that will continue to impact the world for generations, yet he credits golf for getting him through.*

The truth is, this man—although he accomplished so much for the kingdom of God and lived a godly life—faced much opposition, much outright hatred and persecution, and continual financial pressure from all the projects he built for God's work. Golf was a form of play that he enjoyed and that could take his mind off of the daily grind and pressures. It helped him get through.

In his book, *Essentialism*, author Greg McKeown actually shocked me. He spends over two hundred pages talking about how to live as an essentialist and quotes Lin Yutang, saying, "The wisdom of life consists of the elimination of non-essentials."[19] The subtitle says it all, *The Disciplined Pursuit of Less.* He takes twenty chapters to help us unburden ourselves and get rid of things and issues in life that drag us down and complicate our lives. He then spends one whole chapter to argue that *play is essential!* That's what shocked me; however, as I read the chapter, it began to make sense.

McKeown states that play means to "embrace the wisdom of your inner child."[20] He makes the case that as children, we instinctively know how to play, how to be creative, and how to have fun and laugh. However, as we get older, we somehow start to think that play is a waste of time, childish/irresponsible, and unnecessary. As a result, we feel guilty if we want to play golf, tennis, games, or participate in other hobbies. This couldn't be further from the truth.

Stuart Brown actually founded The National Institute for Play, based upon the conclusion from his extensive research that "play has the power to significantly improve everything from personal health to relationships to education to organizations' ability to innovate and stay relevant."[21] I highly recommend that you check out Dr. Brown's website listed in this endnote.

Wow! Let this knowledge motivate you to include play in your regular routines. Find something that makes you smile, that makes you laugh, that takes your mind off of problems and onto *fun*. Like the minister I mentioned, for me, it is golf. I try to play once a week, and each time, I feel refreshed and renewed just from chasing a little white ball around a big field, LOL. Thanks to Mr. McKeown, I am going to keep playing guilt free! I hope you will too.

Vision

Lastly and once again, I want to reiterate the power of vision, or imagination. Can you see yourself happy, carefree, full of joy, peace, and hope for the future? Even if you are hurting so badly that you can only lie in bed and pull the sheets over your head, at least close your eyes and see yourself well—happy, healthy, and hopeful. As Bob Proctor said, "If you can see it in your mind, you can hold it in your hand."[22] Become as a little child. Imagine yourself free!

Vision releases the power to propel you from where you are to where you want to be. Here are three simple steps to help you get started:

- **See it.** Envision yourself with the changes you desire.

- **Feel it**. Experience how it would make you feel to be changed in this way.

- **Get excited!** Speak it, shout it, praise God for it. (Yes, *before* you see it manifested in the natural world. See Romans 4:17.)

If you see yourself as a victim of depression, you will attract continuous episodes. However, if you see yourself as a *victor* over depression, you will attract all you need to live in peace, joy, and hope for a great future.

This may seem oversimplistic, but believe me, it works. It is not a quick fix, and things probably won't change overnight; but if you become as persistent to see yourself happy, whole, and hopeful—as persistent as that dang black dog of depression—I believe you can put him to sleep! This is what I am praying for you. I absolutely believe *we can do it!*

We know for *sure* there is no depression, anxiety, or panic in Heaven, so we can pray, "Father, Thy kingdom come, Thy will be done on earth as it is in Heaven!" *Amen.*

bencares.com

CONCLUSION

ONE CONCEPT I WANT TO LEAVE you with is that of *shalom*. This is one of the most powerful and beautiful words that has ever come to earth. We read in Judges 6:23–24 where this word was spoken to Gideon by the LORD. When Gideon was all concerned about the tumultuous circumstances he was facing, the LORD said, "'Peace [*shalom*] be with you; do not fear, you shall not die.' So Gideon built an altar to the LORD, and called it 'The-LORD-Is-Peace [*shalom*].'" This same word is also used throughout the Old Testament and is a common greeting among Jewish and Arab cultures.

This word is translated "peace" in English, but the word means *so* much more. It means complete wholeness, total prosperity, completeness, nothing missing, nothing broken, all is restored and well! *Shalom* has been described as having three aspects: 1) a heel on the neck of your oppressor, which in effect, takes away the voice of your enemy; 2) anything broken is restored; and 3) anything missing is replaced; all of which bring complete wholeness. So, I speak *shalom*—God's kind of peace—over you, my friend. We stop the voice of the accuser. No more berating the wonderful child of God that you are.

There is something missing if our mind is anxious. A depressed mind is a broken mind, to which *shalom* brings peace and contentment. *Shalom* fills the missing part with wholeness, tranquility, and hope. The revelation of this word actually inspired a song that I have written and recorded.

Yes, my friend, you are a victor, not a victim! You can defeat depression, and I congratulate you on embarking on this journey!

My final word of advice:

SING

My Prayer for You

"Dear Father, I lift up my dear reader. I speak *shalom* over his/her spirit, soul, and body. I pray that You will give him or her wisdom to discover what is causing the mental suffering. I pray that You will send the right people to help him/her find answers. I pray that You will reveal all the knowledge needed to overcome depression and all mental-health issues. I pray that You will fill him/her with hope for a beautiful future and that You will make him or her whole in every way. Amen."

A Prayer for You to Pray

"Father in Heaven, I receive Your love and the gift of salvation. I believe Jesus is Your Son. He died on the cross for my sins, suffered my pain, and bore my sickness and disease. I believe He arose from the dead on the third day and now sits at Your right hand as King of the universe. I receive Your Holy Spirit to help me in life and to defeat depression and anxiety. I give thanks and praise to Your holy name. Amen."

A Note from the Author

Thank you for taking time to walk with me through the pages of this book. I wrote it for you; and I pray that with the grace of God, the help of the Holy Spirit and others, you will silence the black dog that has tormented you. You are in my prayers. Remember, you are a victor not a victim!

Your friend,

Ben Ferrell

P.S. We would love to hear from you and receive your prayer requests. Please write:

Ben Ferrell
Box 55
Oakhurst, OK 74050

Or email me at ben@bencares.com.

HELPFUL RESOURCES

Cecilie Croissant, MA, LPC: https://pathofhopecounseling.com

Dr. Joe Dispenza: https://drjoedispenza.com

Happyfeed.co: This is a good reference with gratitude journals and other mental health resources.

Wim Hof: www.wimhofmethod.com.

National Institute for Play: https://www.nifplay.org

Precision Nutrition: https://www.precisionnutrition.com/blog

Bob Proctor: https://www.proctorgallagherinstitute.com

Dr. Jim Richards: https://drjimrichards.com/ultimate-impact/

Simon Sinek: Leaders Eat Last and https://simonsinek.com/.

Link to my music, a guided meditation, and more: ben-cares.com

My music and guided meditation:

bencares.com

ENDNOTES

[1] United Nations World Health Organization, February 23, 2017. "UN health agency reports depression now 'leading cause of disability worldwide,'" accessed May 26, 2023, https://news.un.org/en/story/2017/02/552062.

[2] Kayla Barnes, August 12, 2021. "The Neuroscience of Gratitude," accessed August 12, 2021, www.byrdie.com.

[3] Neurohealth Associates, July 4, 2020. "Neuroscience Reveals: Gratitude Literally Rewires Your Brain to Be Happier," accessed July 4, 2020, www.nhahealth.com.

[4] Doug Hershey, January 3, 2020. "The True Meaning of Shalom," accessed January 3, 2020, www.firmisrael.org.

[5] Cecilie Croissant, *Enjoying the Journey of Transformation,* (Tulsa, OK: Paladin Publishing, 2021), 85.

[6] Ben Ferrell. "Engaging the Mind of Christ," accessed January 18, 2023, https://www.benferrellmusic.com.

[7] Dr. Alfredo Carpineti, 2017. "Meditation Might Help Reduce Stress Even at a Cellular Level," accessed January 18, 2023, https://www.iflscience.com.

[8] Suruchi Chandra, M.D., n.d. "Neurotherapy: New Paths to Healing," accessed November 1, 2022, https://chandramd.com/neurotherapy-services.

[9] Anna Raab, MA., BCN, nd. Abundant Living Neurofeedback and Counseling, "An Overview," accessed November 1, 2022, https://abundantlivingneuro.com.

[10] Ibid., accessed November 1, 2022, https://abundantlivingneuro.com/reviews/.

[11] "Eye Movement Desensitization and Reprocessing (EMDR) for PTSD," accessed May 24, 2023, https://www.ptsd.va.gov.

[12] Dolores Garcia-Arocena, Ph.D., December 22, 2015. "Happy or SAD? The chemistry behind depression," accessed January 18, 2023, https://www.jax.org.

[13] Stephanie Watson, July 20, 2021. "Oxytocin: the love hormone," accessed January 18, 2023, https://www.health.harvard.edu/mind-and-mood/oxytocin-the-love-hormone.

[14] Ibid., "Serotonin: the natural mood booster," accessed January 18, 2023, https://www.health.harvard.edu/mind-and-mood/serotonin-the-natural-mood-booster.

[15] July 20, 2021. "Endorphins: The brain's natural pain reliever," accessed January 18, 2023, https://www.health.harvard.edu.

[16] Stephanie Watson, July 20, 2021. "Feel-good hormones: How they affect your mind, mood and body," accessed January 18, 2023, https://www.health.harvard.edu/mind-and-mood/feel-good-hormones-how-they-affect-your-mind-mood-and-body.

[17] Osvaldo P. Almeida, January 2, 2018. "B vitamins to enhance treatment response to antidepressants in middle-aged and older adults: results from the B-VINTAGE randomised, double-blind, placebo-controlled trial," accessed January 18, 2023, https://www.cambridge.org.

[18] "5 common foods that can trigger anxiety," accessed January 18, 2023, https://www.intrepidmentalhealth.com.

[19] Greg McKeown, Essentialism: The Disciplined Pursuit of Less, (New York: Currency Publishing, 2014) 83.

[20] Ibid., 83.]

[21] Dr. Stuart Brown, The National Institute for Play, accessed January 20, 2023, https://www.nifplay.org.

[22] Bob Proctor, August 19, 2019. "If You Can See It in Your Mind You Can Hold It in Your Hand," accessed January 20, 2023, https://www.thepeoplealchemist.com.